THE WAY OF THE SUN

THE WAY OF
THE SUN

*White Eagle's teaching for the
festivals of the year*

THE WHITE EAGLE PUBLISHING TRUST
NEW LANDS · LISS · HAMPSHIRE · ENGLAND
MCMLXXXII

First published November 1982
© *The White Eagle Publishing Trust, 1982*
Second impression 1988

White Eagle (*Spirit*)
The way of the Sun.
1. Spirit writings
I. Title
133.9′3   BF1311.W/
ISBN 0–85487–055–5

Printed in Great Britain
at the University Printing House, Oxford
by David Stanford
Printer to the University

CONTENTS

v

vi

Introduction

IN THIS book we print a selection of teaching given by White Eagle at times of the year's festivals. He speaks of the inner meaning of the festivals, and sometimes more generally of the seasons in which they fall. The book covers the Christian celebrations of Easter, Whitsun, Remembrance and Christmas; but also those natural times of festival associated with the passage of the seasons, especially the times of equinox and solstice. In fact White Eagle associates the Christian anniversaries with the great natural rhythm of the year, and sees all the festivals as times when we have an opportunity to be touched by a special blessing of spiritual life; to share in fuller consciousness the life of the spiritual sun.

A few words may be helpful to introduce the way White Eagle talks of the natural cycle of the year in various places in the book. At the present time our own lives are not outwardly so governed by the changing seasons as would have been the case before the advent of industrial civilisation. Even more we have lost the habit of inner attunement to the natural rhythm of the year that some great civilisations of the past—for instance, that of the American Indian —have had; and the increased ability to hold communion with the divine life, the Great Spirit, that went hand in hand with this attunement. White Eagle talks in the section on Harvest of the relationship felt by ancient peoples with the great Mother, Mother Earth, who was responsible for the production of all physical form, and all the gifts of nature. This attunement to the life of nature, far from limiting their awareness to the physical world, increased their ability to live in communion with the divine life behind all physical form.

The cycle of the year brought times when there was a special attunement between the world of nature and the divine life of which the physical sun was an outward symbol. Man, sharing the life of nature, could at these times be particularly helped to draw close to the spiritual sun: the source of life and warmth, light, love and strength—to God. These were accordingly periods for festival. The winter solstice, for instance, is the point of the apparent 'rebirth' of the physical sun in the cold of winter, when the life of nature is quiescent and withdrawn; it is the first sign of the coming return of warmth and growth to the earth. White Eagle has said that this was for peoples of the past an occasion of physical celebration, and of co-operation with the invisible forces of nature. But it was also a festival of the birth of the light of the spiritual sun in matter—and for the birth of this light and consciousness in the heart of man. The people worshipped and held communion with the light that was behind all physical life; they were able to receive a special blessing and increase of awareness. Through the ensuing months the apparent gathering of the sun's strength brings a great outbreathing of life in nature which reaches its climax at midsummer. This time of the fullest flowering of nature—at the summer solstice and the full moon preceding it—was again one of physical celebration, before that which had been sown was reaped in beauty; but it was a festival too of physical life being brought to perfection and glorified by the spirit: a time when the rhythm of nature helped man to realise the presence of the great spirit of love within his own heart, and its power to redeem and irradiate his whole being.

The Christian festivals as kept in the modern world are outwardly unconnected with those that arose from living close to nature, but it is one of the beauties of White Eagle's teaching in this book that in a simple and illuminating way he shows that there is a harmony between them. It is beyond coincidence, for instance, that the traditional time of the major Christian festival, Christmas, almost coincides with the winter solstice in the northern hemisphere. Christmas, of course, celebrates the birth of Jesus; but as we worship at the birthplace of Christ we are also worshipping before the Christ light that lies deep within our own being: the light of the Son of God, the spiritual Sun, the spirit of love that has to be born into the earthly personality of every man. Even the very recent institution of the day of Remembrance, which

3

falls close to the older commemoration of All Souls, comes at a significant season. Autumn is the period when the life of nature withdraws from outer manifestation; it remains hidden, awaiting the next outbreathing in the spring. But this withdrawal of life in nature from the outer form can subtly help us become aware of the closeness of the unseen world, the world of spirit. At All Souls and at Remembrance, when the lives of those who have passed into the world of spirit are commemorated, the rhythm of the year itself helps bring a close communion with those who have left the physical body and passed on to freedom and further work.

White Eagle says that the purpose of man's life on earth is to help him to grow spiritually: gradually to develop the consciousness of God through the discipline of earthly experience. Man does this through daily life; and there may be those who feel that awareness of the festivals mentioned in this book has only a very little part to play in a man's aspiration to the Christ light. It is true that it is what is done every day that makes festivals significant. White Eagle's gentle human teaching, printed in this book as specially appropriate to the various festivals and seasons, is helpful at any time of the year. But this is not quite the whole picture.

It is easy to feel, for instance, how a natural thankfulness for the enjoyment of physical life brought by a particular time of year—the perfect flowering of nature in the summer, the human love and companionship felt at Christmas—opens one's heart to the spiritual life that encompasses the physical level. White Eagle himself says, 'When the human heart is open in thankfulness for all the gifts of life, something happens. You feel happy, you feel at peace, you begin to be relaxed from the stresses and burdens of your earthly life; you come nearer to an understanding of life, of eternal life. This is why it is a good thing to hold these harvest festivals, to hold a Christmas festival, to hold a spring festival.' Festivals are times when the spirit of thankfulness opens man's spiritual senses.

The celebration too of the Christian festivals, even if simply in memory of the life of Jesus, can bring the mystical truths symbolised by these festivals very close. There can be no time when it is easier to understand the words, *Except ye . . . become as little children, ye shall not enter into the kingdom of heaven*, than at Christmas, centred on the image of the Christ child: the Christ child that is also the Christ love born in the human heart.

But alongside this, there is also the reason for festivals discussed earlier. We do not now live so attuned to the rhythm and movement of nature as some civilisations of the past. Yet man's fundamental make-up has not changed; and White Eagle has said that in the Aquarian Age he will again become more sensitive to the great Mother, Mother Earth; and to the way the earthly seasons, governed by the physical sun, can attune him to the light and joy of the great spiritual Sun: his true heritage of eternal life.

We hope that White Eagle's loving words will help those who read them find their own happiness.

A.J.H.
July 1982

I

The New Year

A Happy New Year

W HEN each New Year comes it is the custom for you to wish each other happiness, health and success; for then everyone feels in his heart that a fresh page is opening, with the past relegated to the background. You hope that in this New Year your life will develop harmoniously and happily. Hope springs eternal in the human heart, because it is of the spirit. The spirit, which is the Son of God, is eternal; and because it is eternal it always speaks to the soul of hope, of happiness.

Therefore, we in spirit come back to bring you a message of hope and to urge you to think always in terms of love, goodwill and happiness; and by doing this you will create for yourselves your own heaven— heaven within your soul, and your heaven in the world of spirit, which is your true home.

We would remind you that human life is governed by spiritual law, by the law of cause and effect and also by the law of opportunity. In the East the first is called 'karma', the second, 'dharma'. You do not fully understand what these two laws mean in daily life. Now you have been given the gift of freewill, and many people feel that because they have freewill they are their own masters, and can do as they like. This is true. Nevertheless, the soul must be prepared to face the result of its actions. That is, if it chooses the way of selfishness and unkindness it must be prepared to suffer the effects which will follow upon that desire.

However the law of cause and effect goes hand in hand with the law of opportunity. Each time a cause is sown, like a seed, in the individual, or in the national or international life, there is bound to be a following effect, which can be either happy or unhappy. But, in any case it will bring fresh opportunity, for the law of karma causes the law of dharma or opportunity to operate. In sorrow and in joy, remember that the outworking of your karma is bringing you an opportunity to acquire wisdom and thus step forward on the path.

As you aspire towards God, as you endeavour to let the divine light within expand and grow so that all your thoughts are positive and good, all your aspirations are heavenward, you will set in motion vibrations of power. You will yourself become a vortex of spiritual light and power, and you will command— even unconsciously—all good. Your life will then take on a new aspect. You will first begin to feel a quiet harmony within, a certain confidence in God. To know God is to have faith that all things are working together for good in your life, that all things will work together for good in the world. The cycle of life is moving upwards in a spiral. In spite of patches of darkness, which you call evil, mankind is progressing. A heavenly light is penetrating men's minds, and the hearts of men and women are opening, reaching out towards love, goodwill, righteousness.

We in spirit can look upon the earth from an angle which you cannot. We can see into the hearts of people, and what we see is beautiful. We see goodness, we see the light of Christ growing. We also see that which is crying out for love, and this is where you can help. Remember, God has endowed you with the qualities of His Son, the Christ. You have the power within to create your own heaven and to create your own hell; to create heaven or to create hell for your brother man.

And so we say, in this New Year, look to the spirit; let the spirit guide you in all your undertakings. Be true to your innermost light, and you will create heaven and know complete happiness on earth. Do not dismiss what we say with the excuse that it is no use only one person making the effort. The way to bring a golden age on earth is for every individual to be true to the light of the spirit of Christ within them. Put this into practice in your lives, and you will be amazed at the results.

Looking forward positively

In your own lives always look forward, anticipate good. By anticipating good, by anticipating blessings and happiness, you are actually drawing these to you; you are creating, through your imagination. Imagination is part of the psychic gift implanted in man's soul. Therefore, we say to you from spirit, *use* your heavenly imagination; imagine yourself in a state of perfect health, imagine yourself in a state of harmony. If your conditions are inharmonious, see them becoming smoother, better. Disciplined imagination is the key to creation.

Perhaps you are unaware that whenever you think negatively, you are actually creating negative conditions for yourselves. To create positive good, you must always think positively. If you do this habitually you will clear the mists which gather round you— mists in your own soul, mists in your mind. The light of Christ in you, expressing itself through your positive thinking, can shine like a sun and dispel the mists.

We cannot impress upon you too strongly to think always in terms of progress, of happiness and of achievement; and you will become healthy and happy. This is our special message for you as you stand at the beginning of a new year. For as you *image* your conditions so you are setting into operation the machinery which will bring about the very picture you hold in your mind. As you *think* light, as you think good, you will become a creator, with God, of a beautiful world, a beautiful humanity.

With Vision on the Star

We give you a very simple message which we hope will help you. Do you remember Jesus speaking of putting your hand to the plough and not looking back? The ploughman ploughs a straight furrow by fixing his gaze on a marking post; and so we say keep your vision on the marking post, the guiding post. The post we give you reaches high, far above the earth. And upon that post is a glorious six-pointed star, symbol of man perfected, the Christed man. You can never go wrong if you give your heart to that symbol of the six-pointed star. It will never misguide you, never mislead you. It will guide you through your life, right up to the golden world of God. The golden world of God is the world of spirit, and this world of spirit is not only somewhere 'up there' in the spheres, it is also here, on earth.

You are here in a physical body on the earth to do God's work. What is this work, you may ask? It is to live in obedience to the law of God in every detail of your life, and thus eventually to establish the kingdom of God upon earth. By the kingdom of God we mean a state of life where humanity has fully learnt the law of brotherhood. Think what this means! To be truly well and happy and live in the kingdom of God man must live, think and act purely; and his bodies, etheric, astral, mental, celestial, all must be perfected and purified by the guiding spirit of God, that invisible light, that pure radiant light above and within him. The symbol of this light is the six-pointed star.

When, in spite of frustration and loss and disappointment and grief, man can keep on keeping

11

bravely on the path, holding fast to belief in the love of his Father–Mother, the Great White Spirit, he cannot but enter into the golden world of inner peace and ineffable happiness.

Remember, as you step forward on your journey through life, that above you is this illimitable star of heavenly light, like a ray from God's heart shining into you, and it will guard and guide you until your journey's end. Wherever you are, whatever you are doing, God is with you and you can be working for God. The Great White Spirit looks upon you with loving graciousness and bids you live in the reflection of His light. Never doubt God's care for you, and that by His will the spirit messengers, guides and loved ones are taking care of you. Meditate daily on the Christ star in the heavens. See its heavenly light shining upon the earth, into the heart and mind of every man, woman and child, inspiring and guiding humanity. See its rays penetrating the darkness, until the whole earth becomes illumined by the Christ light —the second coming of Christ to earth.

At the Beginning of Spring: Man's Heavenly Senses

When a flower grows in Mother Earth, when a tree, a young sapling, begins to grow, it has to face the buffeting of physical forces—the wind, the heat of the sun, drought and storm—and the ignorance of man. So too is man buffeted, and he has to become strong in his effort to grow out of the dark soil and reach up to the light of the gentle sun's rays. Life, dear brethren, is effort; and spiritual life too means effort. So you must not become complacent, you must reach up all the time.

Think of the great trees that have grown from a tiny seed; think of the corn that has grown from the little golden grain and of the bread which supplies your daily need. Think of the water which falls by command of the Creator. Never grumble, dear brethren, about rainy days! Welcome them, for they are cleansing, they are refreshing. Never grumble about the rain; never grumble about the air currents and the wind, even if it is uncomfortable and buffets you. We speak of your spiritual life as well as your physical. Welcome the brothers of the air; welcome the brothers of the sun.

Oh brethren, in our life on earth, in the woods and by the running river where we lived with our people, we found that intense peace and happiness which you in your present life so often miss. We advise you, when you are troubled in mind, to walk in your garden, walk over the soft turf, look at the blades of grass . . . they are part of you because you are part of God, you are part of the sun. You could not live without the sun, or the water, or the air, or the earth; nor can you live spiritually without bridging the etheric gap by the senses of your soul. The sense of sound, for instance—sound . . . what does sound mean to you? Listen to the sound of God, the Word of God, to the great Aum . . . Aum . . . Aum . . . which is all around you, catching you up in its infinite power.

In the beginning was the Word and the Word was with God . . .; and all these sounds—the sound of music, of the wind in the trees, the running water, the quiet breathing of the earth—are stimulating in the soul an awareness of heaven. Across this etheric bridge of sound, of music, you are carried into our Sun Temple. We say our Sun Temple because all brethren know that their true home is above, in the Sun Temple in the heavens, and all your thoughts which reach that height bring back to the little you on earth new life from your Creator, the power of creating new life in your body, in your soul. The power of thought, brethren, takes you anywhere. Call it imagination if you like, but see beyond your imagination into the glory of God's heaven, because it is only by your heavenly vision, your heavenly hearing, that you will reach that Temple of the Sun.

Now, brethren, use your imagination. Feel yourself being caught up in this creative note—call it the great Amen if you will, but the ancients knew it as the great Aum of life, and it sweeps you up across the etheric bridge into your true home, your eternal home.

Use your imagination and see that you are in this grand Sun Temple where the lifegiving rays of the sun are enveloping you and holding you firmly and strongly. . . .

This is what mankind needs: light, sun, air, water, and the stimulation of all the gifts of the soul, for the

14

soul is man's bridge between earth and heaven.

May the feelings of your soul be pure and loving and happy and aspiring, and then you will go up and across the bridge, which reaches right up into the heart of the loving God.

Seek this consciousness of the truth, the light, the life. . . .

To See with Eyes freed from Confusion

Whatever problem you now face, face it in the light of Christ, and do not allow thoughts of fear or misunderstanding to cramp and blind you. Look into the face of the master, the gentle wise elder brother, and strive daily to live in thought, in company with him. And you will find that conditions will be made clear for you, the path before you will be straightened out. Strive to live above the materiality of the world.

There are two strata of life: the earth plane, where there is darkness and confusion, and above, the land of light, wherein you may dwell if you turn your back upon the error and darkness of the material level of life, and concentrate heart and mind upon the land of light. Do not think that this is a land of illusion, for it is real, and by living with your head in the sunshine (not in the clouds!) you will be living in a land of reality. We do not want our earthly brethren to have their heads in clouds, we want them to have their heads in the sunlight. It does not render a man impractical to live in this way. On the contrary, it makes

15

him more efficient, with all his senses bright, and gives him clarity of thought. Keep your head in the sunlight, and your feet upon beloved Mother Earth, walking the green carpet of earth, so soft and springy, which is comforting, which is homely.

May your life be like this! And it can be. It does not depend upon outer conditions, poverty or wealth, friendship or companionship. It depends only upon you and your relationship with . . . the light of God. You will have all things if you will become *truly* at one with love, which is Christ. *I, if I be lifted up from the earth, will draw all men unto me.* Raise the Christ in yourself, and all men with whom you associate will be lifted up with you, and you will see them, not as enemies, but as simple, dear kindly brothers. It is not they who are your enemies. No, beloved child, it is *you* that have failed to raise yourself to the beloved . . . Christ.

The Perspective of the Mind of the Spirit

Do your best, and your little problems (which may appear to be very big to you but they are only small problems) will all be overcome; have patience, and faith in the Great White Spirit, and your problems will all be overcome. This does not mean that you must be slack and not do your best—but don't do it feverishly, do it patiently and trustingly. You can work yourself into a fever, and suffer; or you can remain calm and tranquil and happy. Not easy, we know, but this is all part of your training. Can you imagine the one whom you love and trust as your master getting feverishly anxious or upset? We say this to you: place your whole confidence in God. God knows your need. God will enfold and protect you if you surrender your will to His divine wisdom.

II

Spring and Easter

Open your Heart to the Sun

IN THE PAST, ceremonies were held at this time of the year, when the sun was returning with its warmth and life-force to bring forth from the earth itself the manifestation of God's life and beauty. We would raise your consciousness beyond the darkness of the earth life, and bring you a vision of the company of radiant spirits and angels who draw near to your earth at this time in obedience to the law, to the will of our Father–Mother God. They come amongst you with rejoicing, trying to infuse into your being the joy of the sunlight, the joy of the Christ life. They try to awaken in your soul and higher consciousness supreme confidence in God's love and wisdom. You may, if you will, receive the baptism of this Sun spirit, even as the brethren of the ancient wisdom have always received it.

Turn your back, beloved brethren, on the darkness and error of mortal thinking. On the lower mental plane there is confusion, and the man who dwells in the prison house of the flesh dwells in confusion. But the spirit within him aspires and reaches forth to its Father–Mother God, and cries out in joy that it lives

18

and has its true being in the heaven world.

In this modern age, you have lost touch with the truth of being in God's light and beauty and good. Brotherhood is hardly known. But at this time of the festival of the arisen Sun, let us all make a supreme effort to open our hearts to God, the great Sun of all life, and reflect its light into the hearts of men. So may we become brothers to all life, simple, gentle and true, so that if God wills He may use any one of us to comfort, inspire and heal our fellows.

The ancient festival of welcoming the sun at this season of the year will be revived when men realise the true art of life. The Sun of God (by which we mean the life-force which flows from the heart of God, which is love) will enter in fullness and richness into man's being in the same way as the sun enters into the seed quickened to life in Mother Earth. As nature is quickened by the same force of love, so man will be quickened and grow to perfection. There will be in those days not stricken men and women, but all will be as perfect sons of God.

We believe in the coming of the brotherhood of Christ on earth. We work for this end.

True Nutriment for Crops

Looking back, my brethren, down our path of life, we have a memory, the picture of an ancient American life—of a time when the brethren understood and worshipped the Great White Spirit. Because they had touched the centre of life they comprehended the power in that life and in the light. They knew that the earth needed food, and without a supply of the heavenly food would become exhausted. And so these ancient Indian brethren used to gather on the plain and invoke the blessing of the Almighty Spirit.

They grew their food with knowledge and understanding not only of physical but of spiritual law. They did not stimulate the earth artificially, but grew their food amid natural conditions and called down on the earth the great white light, this wonderful element of the light which is love, to stimulate life in the earth.

Now, brethren, that same white light, about which mankind today knows so little, can still be called down, gathered into the earth to give nutriment, not only to help the grain to burst and send forth its shoot; but also to make it grow to perfection. Those of you who have gardens, and who are lovers of nature, will ponder on what we say. The finest food that you can give to your crops is the great white light, the love of God.

Resurrection

Now is a time of resurrection, resurrection from darkness and the cold of wintertime into a golden spring. How thankfully you greet the sun in your northern hemisphere as the days grow longer and brighter after the drear cold. This is an illustration of what takes place in the soul of man when he can attune himself to the warmth and the love and the light of the spiritual sun, and free himself from his enslavement by physical matter. We are not suggesting that the physical life is unimportant. The physical life on your earth is of the utmost importance. But man has been put into a physical body in order to learn to free himself from the bondage of matter and to fill the physical life with the beauty, happiness, well-being and health that God intends him to have. In other words, to attain mastery over physical matter. By self-discipline, by subjugation of the lower instincts the selfishness which is in the flesh, and man can be reborn into the spirit. In time the spirit will command the whole earth and the golden age will come on earth.

The golden age! At this time of the year, in the spring time when the sun shines, bringing warmth and lightness and joy to the earth, nature bursts forth into golden flower, and green-gold leaf—a reflection of that lovely golden spiritual sunlight which radiates from the Christos. You have no conception of the beauty of that golden light radiating from the Lord Christ, which shines forth like a blazing star all over the earth.

Have you ever noticed that so many of the spring flowers which push through Mother Earth at Easter time, the daffodil, the hyacinth and many others, manifest the symbol of the six-pointed star? They have six petals; and deep within the flower you will see yet another little star in many of them. Just examine your spring flowers and you will see there the message of the arisen Christ, for the six-pointed star is the symbol of man and God united. God manifesting through man. Man made perfect through the gentle Christ spirit within his being. My children, when you release yourselves from the bondage of earth, of materialism, you will not only recognise the Christ spirit in the world of spirit, but you will also recognise it down on your earth. But your recognition of it depends on you and on your own way of life, your own spiritual development, the unfolding of that flower of the divine spirit within you.

Throughout the ages there have been Christed ones, men made perfect by the Christ spirit within; men who have learnt the secret of the Christ being. But Jesus above all, through his life, death and resurrection, demonstrated the power of God which was within him and within every man, to transfigure, to transform, to irradiate matter. Did he not say, *He that believeth on me, the works that I do shall he do also; and greater works than these shall he do . . .*? Every man has this gift within him, but the creative power which man has to change himself, to change the world, is not loud, noisy, and quarrelsome—it is the humble, gentle, loving spirit. It is the gentle spirit of Christ which you all have within you which is the power that performs miracles.

This, my children, is what will save mankind, not

the crucifixion of the Master on a cross, but the crucifixion of the lower self and the release of the glorious son of God in man. Eastertide is not the celebration of death and physical crucifixion; it is the celebration of life and resurrection, an awakening from materiality into the beauty and wonder of the spiritual life—not after the death of the physical body, but whilst you are still living on this beautiful earth, in this beautiful world which God, the first great cause of life, has created.

Surrender

Beloved brethren, your religion teaches you to feel unhappy at this glorious time of the year, and many are heavy with sorrow at the thought of the crucifixion of their lord and Master; they think sorrowfully of the physical body suffering on a cross. May we tell you that the crucifixion is not as you understand it. It is a symbol of the spiritual growth and evolution of man, the symbol of the initiation of the earth, and in it can be read the story of the liberation of the spirit from the domination of the flesh and earthly matter.

The beloved Master Jesus could not be crucified nor put to the agony which men imagine. He withdrew from his physical body, and could not be harmed through any physical ordeal. This is a great truth that you too have to learn, that the spirit of man can be touched neither by pain nor grief nor sorrow.

The lower nature, the self which is full of pride,

resents having to surrender to the will of the Father; and so long as it resents it suffers. You have experienced this in your own life. You are in this sense crucified in matter, and you suffer; but as soon as you surrender to the will of God, your suffering ceases.

This is a lesson which Easter has to teach. It is a time of sweet surrender to the light and beauty of the spirit; and with this surrender comes the great outpouring from the Son, Christ, to bless the child of God.

The crucifixion is a symbol of the earth initiation in which (put in very simple language) the soul, having seen the glory of the Father, is able to demonstrate that glory in his actions on earth. It is one thing to know theoretically, but practice is very far from theory. The earth initiation means bringing the Christ spirit into manifestation in daily life.

Whatever your personal sorrow, fix your vision upon the glorious light of God and you shall have peace in your heart and you will rejoice, for the love of God will be made plain to you. Do not let your mind batter at you with trivial questions. Rather cultivate steadfast faith in goodness and in evolution. Cultivate a very steady and calm mind and a heart full of love towards God and your fellow man.

My children, when the inrush of God's love comes to you, as a natural happening, you will know weariness neither of mind, body nor spirit. You will say, 'Oh, that belief is all very well for you, White Eagle!' But do not forget that we too have passed along the

24

same road as do you. We know the weakness and weariness of the flesh, but we know that you can only arrive at constant renewal by cultivating awareness and faith in God.

The Arisen Christ

The message for which all the world is waiting is that of the arisen Christ. When this message from the spirit is heard by the world humanity will receive the full power of the spiritual Sun, of the arisen Christ.

During the Christian era men have studied the message of the Master Jesus, but they have not comprehended its full implication. Man does not even understand *why* he is on earth; nor does he know that he came from realms supernal—that is, that his spirit as a divine spark came from realms of light. If man once understood the purpose of his life here, and the whole story of his spiritual birth, evolution and resurrection, he would turn his face to the light; and instead of dwelling on the form of the crucified man, he would see a risen sun; and in the heart of that sun would see the Perfect One, the son of man and the Son of God. He would see that form with arms outstretched making a cross of light within the circle of light, and he would be seeing his goal, the end of all his travail. Then would he be inspired by the divine love of the Christ spirit.

We would like you, dear brethren, to hold in your mind's eye this picture that we have drawn of the perfect man—of Jesus standing with arms out-stretched in the golden Sun, which represents all life. For behind the physical sun shines a spiritual glory which is its real life, essence and power. What we have to tell you is that every man and woman born of flesh has deep within him this same light of the Sun, and when he wills may draw it to himself in ever-increasing measure. He can also breathe in this life-force. He can absorb it in the water he drinks, in the air he breathes, in the pure food he consumes. He can absorb this spiritual life-force in full consciousness, and it will cause him to grow in spirit and glory until his whole being radiates the light as did that symbolic form which we have given you, of Jesus in the Sun—the picture of the arisen Christ.

But something has to happen before man is resurrected from darkness to light, from death to life. When you live in the spirit, life is eternal; but the first step for man to take is to work through the bondage of his limiting flesh and to realise that his spiritual life is an eternal life. In spirit there is no death, no separation from love or loved ones. There is no time when you have not *been*, and there will be no time when you will not *be*. Someone has asked: 'Shall we eventually be absorbed into the infinite light and glory of God, and so lose our individuality?' We say that as you develop and grow in the Christ life you will become ever more and more individualised, but you will also become more and more absorbed into the infinite glory which you worship as God. Cannot you see that the more the Christ in man grows, the more Godlike he becomes? The more beautiful his form and life, the more certain it is that he will retain his individuality. But he will also so radiate the life of the Christ that he will become at one with the Father.

Jesus continually said: 'The Father and I are one'. He tried always to teach the world the deep truth that within man is God. But man has been given freewill. He can allow God to develop, he can encourage the growth of Christ, within him; or, alternatively, he can by his own immersion in selfishness reject this very growth.

Understand that life itself is the Son in you, and the Son is the Christ spirit. The real *you*, the essence of you, my brother, my sister, is part of the Christ spirit, for *you* are not the little earthly personality that you think you are. You came from God, you are part of God, you are God's seed. Within the seed of the plant is stored the beauty of the flower, the richness of the fruit.

This seed or spark has enfolded itself through the ages with wrapping upon wrapping of earthly clothing, until it is wrapped up so tightly that it can hardly breathe. But it has to go through this process of involution for a purpose, and that purpose is growth and acquisition of knowledge—so that in due time it can burst its shell of darkness and can be reborn to rise on wings of light. This is the meaning of the ancient symbolism of the white eagle, of the phoenix, of the Egyptian sphinx, and of winged images of stone which are found in many parts of the earth. These are to indicate that man has the power within him to rise into higher worlds, into higher states of life; for even as a bird can rise and fly through the air, so can man rise in spirit to higher realms of life and consciousness.

A master is one who has by hard work and self-discipline and divine love in himself—and in giving his divine love, giving all gentleness and kindness to his brethren—attained to a degree of mastery of matter. You too have to learn how to rise in spirit and command the flesh.

You are now in the process of crucifixion. It is very painful, your life may be hard, you get weary of the burden, and the cross you bear is more than you can stand sometimes; but it is only the power of the spirit of Christ within you that will enable you to rise and carry that burden as though it did not exist. This is for you, it is for everyone on this earth plane, to understand, and to set to work to develop more and more this divine love in the heart.

Through development of divine love in the heart, wisdom comes, knowledge comes. With the coming of knowledge and wisdom and love the whole being of man will be suffused with the power of heaven.

The work of man's spirit here is so to purify the flesh that there is no disease, no corruption. The body is purified by the power of God within, so that when at death the lower form is shed, the form of the perfect one, the soul and the body of purified atoms, lives on, as Jesus demonstrated. As man purifies his life by divine love and wisdom, and by service to his brother man, so his physical body will become refined and rarified and his body will become so pure that he enters into the world of spirit without corruption of the flesh.

Men make the mistake of saying there is no life after death, because in their darkness they cannot see into that unseen world of rarified life. But that world is there and it is eternal. It is this world of matter which is corruptible; but that world which is created from the light of God, and is God, remains eternal.

You move forward. You are now going up the arc on your return journey to that place of perfect life. The Christ within you will rise, and you will be perfected in his glory.

The Golden Flowers of Easter

Spiritual truth, and indeed all truth, must be acceptable to both the heart and to the mind. Some people think that love is purely an emotion and that therefore the voice of love cannot satisfy their reason; but love in its divine sense completely satisfies. And when fully developed in man it can raise him from the valley to the heights, giving him a range of vision which is only possible from the apex of the mountain.

Do not think that the festival of Easter belongs exclusively to Christianity, for it is ages old, and the

29

story embodied in the Christian teaching is yet another enactment of the mystical story of Christ the Sun.

It is not easy for you today to associate the Cosmic Christ with the sun in the skies, although you regard the sun as the source of the warmth and light without which there could be no life on earth. At Easter time, when the great sun pours forth its rays upon the northern hemisphere, all life begins to stir. Most of the early spring flowers in the northern hemisphere take upon themselves the colour of the sun. Does not this sun-colour stimulate your intellect and warm your heart? Your hearts leap when you see the little golden flowers raising their heads from the dark earth and turning their faces to the sun; for then all nature is stirring and rising to glorify the Creator. All will admit that there is a natural law behind this awakening life and growth.

But there is something more; there is a divine Intelligence; and more even than this, there is a great warm Heart. Have you ever thought of the warmth of the heart of God, the heart of your Creator? Come with us then; rise in consciousness above physical matter, into the realms of the Sun or of the spirit . . . Feel the warmth and glory and life-giving power of the Sun . . . and then know that something of this Sun, or spirit is also in your heart. For within man's heart is a tiny replica of the Sun, of the heart of God the Creator; and God and Christ are one.

If you remember this, it will help you not only to

unfold your own Sun qualities or Christ qualities but to comprehend the purpose of life here on this earth.

How are you, as an individual, going to bring into your life the power and the life of the Cosmic Christ? First, by remembering that Christ is not some remote being whom you will meet some day, if you are good enough, after you have passed away from the earth and through the planes of life surrounding the earth. No, Christ is an ever-present power and intelligence, Christ is a friend, a brother to you *now*—if you so wish. He is also a saviour. We are not speaking so much of the human Master, Jesus; we are speaking of the cosmic and mystical glory which has been since the beginning of life on this planet, and yet which is so comprehending and understanding of man's nature and needs that he can and does take upon himself a form like man's form. It is very important for you to realise that this Being of light and glory can come to you in a human form, understanding human and personal problems, understanding your perplexity, your fears, your grief, your loneliness.

Today man has developed mentally, but lacking wisdom has neither humility nor simplicity in his heart to comprehend the beauty and the glory of his Creator's love. If some day you think you have seen a vision of the Christ Being, or of the Master Jesus, this is not mere imagination. Jesus also was not separate from the world's humanity, but had learnt to live the perfect life of love, and had realised his at-one-ment with his Creator. His soul was prepared for his great mission and he was sent to this earth to be used by Christ, the Son of God, to bring the truth about their salvation to earthly people; so that they could see the power of the Son in man.

'Salvation' is the true word to describe the mission of the Christ spirit; for when the Christ spirit becomes alive in man, man is literally saved from his sins; he lives in the light, and brings the light into the world. Once the Christ spirit quickens within him, the world can no longer touch him. This is what salvation means—not salvation through belief in one particular man, but salvation by reason of the Christ love within man himself. This will forbid him to wage war against his brother or to treat his brother as less than himself; but will inspire him to words and actions of kindness and consideration, to work for God in his daily life, to live in consciousness of a glory which is above, around and within him, and in all life. This is salvation by Christ. Always the Lord of this earth, the Sun, the Son who is the saviour of mankind, quickens the life of the spirit in man.

So, children of earth, we raise your consciousness to that Christ Sun which is all love, wisdom and strength. If you wish to be attuned to that Source, you must live a life of loving service, thinking kindly, ever believing the best, ever being patient, cherishing a faith which is an inner knowing that you are God's child. He will never fail you, but you must never fail Him. The glory of Eastertide be upon you in full

32

measure. May your heart rise in praise and thanksgiving, and the blessing of the Almighty Spirit be upon you all.

III

The Wesak Festival and Whitsun

THE WESAK FESTIVAL

When Easter, the great festival of the arisen Sun, has passed, it is for a time as if a quietness settles upon the earth. In spite of all the lush new growth and the activity of the new-born life, there is felt a deep underlying peace which we associate with the divine Mother aspect of God, who gives form to all beauty.

It is at this time that the Buddhist festival of Wesak occurs, not only on the outer planes when disciples and followers of the Lord Buddha are drawn together in a great festival of communion and reunion and worship; but more vitally in the inner ethers, which White Eagle describes as a 'meeting place between heaven and earth'. And at that level a ceremony takes place through which the influence of the compassionate Buddha blesses the whole earth.

The meditation at this time is of utter stillness and surrender, and of the oneness of all life; those who can tune in to the festival and share the great communion can, in meditation, reflect into the world the deep peace of the Lord Buddha and the shining brotherhood gathered there.

White Eagle tells us that the Wesak festival is, in a sense, a time of preparation. 'It is a period of stillness and preparation of the mind and heart for the next great spiritual outpouring, the Christ festival, which comes at the full moon which falls when the sun is in Gemini. Then a festival is held in the spirit realms, a ceremony at which the Lord Christ comes amongst His disciples and pours a special blessing, a tremendous outpouring of love, upon the earth, which is light and truth and beauty, it is spiritual food. The ceremony is as old as earth itself.'

Although both the Wesak and the Christ festivals fall at the full moon, the spiritual influence from them is felt for a few days before the full moon, and lasts for many days afterwards. The Christ festival is linked with the Christian festival of Whitsun, and the influence from it can be felt right through to the summer solstice.

The Message of the Lord Buddha

THE LORD Buddha brought to mankind the message of peace and brotherhood. He brought the message of stillness. We are going to suggest to you that the Lord Buddha, in bringing the message of peace, taught man how to prepare the way for the coming of the Christ. He taught his disciples how to meditate and become conscious of the enfolding power of God; he taught them how to live wisely in brotherhood, and to understand the sufferings of those on earth. He gave them compassion. He explained to them that if they were able to touch the infinite stillness, the source of true life and power,

35

they would not suffer; and that all men can live in that state of spiritual life without suffering. So Buddha pointed the way, prepared the minds, for the baptism of the Christ light.

And now at this present time, as they are advancing into the Aquarian Age, men all over the world are receiving guidance. The light is descending and permeating the lives of countless men and women all over the world, as part of a natural process of spiritual evolution. And the way man prepares his consciousness to receive the blessing, the way he develops his ability to contact invisible worlds, is by training himself to become still, still in mind and body. In this state of meditation, in this stillness and silence, the Lord comes.

Every man must walk his own path, but every man can be helped by his companions. When you sit in contemplation and meditation, although you may prefer to be alone, indeed you always *are* alone in your own inner sanctuary, you cannot really dwell in splendid isolation and apart from your brethren. Through meditation and contemplation of God, you find unity with all God's creatures. This is the goal.

It is at this point, being raised in consciousness to an awareness of God in all men and all men in God, that man receives the baptism of the holy fire. The light, the 'tongues of fire' descend and rest upon his head, bringing him illumination. The man so illumined feels and knows the power of the Holy Spirit. His vision and understanding are quickened and his one desire is to help and care for his brethren, whatever their experiences on earth. Thereafter he lives not for himself, but that his life may bless others.

When man receives the holy blessing, he is then an ambassador of God, and goes forth into life to serve, to uplift, to heal, to comfort. He is a chosen one of God in the service of man, even as the apostles after Pentecost.

This thought we would commend to you, that the development of your own being is not for your own sake, but so that you can render service to life, so that you can more adequately give.

We leave you with all love, and the blessing of the Great White Spirit. . . .

A Meditation for the Wesak Festival

We would raise you from your lower physical level of thought to the upper level, to the purer air, to the finer pulsation or vibration of life. We would take you to the vast assembly of brethren on the higher etheric plane, the assembly of the Buddhist or Wesak festival of peace, compassion and love. In your heart, in your pure spirit, you will be enveloped in this sweet and holy love . . . your own heart must be full of love and compassion for all life, for at this level brothers of the light know that all life is one. You feel compassion for all life: for the animal kingdom, the nature king-

37

dom, even for the mineral kingdom and for the very substance of the earth planet.

Meditate on this at-one-ment. . . .

In the holy silence, see, see with your inner vision the form of the Lord Buddha; with him is the Master Jesus and behind both these forms the perfect shining golden figure of the Cosmic Christ. As you become absorbed into this golden light you feel especially the contact with the Lord Buddha as he pours forth the blessing of love and compassion upon all life.

Peace, infinite peace fills your soul.

All discordant feelings and thoughts are washed away in this divine peace and the radiance of the Lord Buddha. It waxes and then it wanes, like a great cosmic breath, and as the radiance glows from his form you feel the infinite peace enfolding you and find yourself breathing forth peace and love on all living creatures.

You are now with the great brotherhood of the ages in the temple of the one true light, the Christos.

Feel the perfect harmony in this universal temple of brotherhood. Feel the rhythm of all life, the at-one-ment of all the kingdoms of life from the amoeba, through all the kingdoms, right to the supreme Being. Feel the rhythm, the lifebeat of all creatures . . . Feel the complete at-one-ment of all life. . . .

Worship in your own way in the temple of universal brotherhood. You are in IT, you are in this vast sea of life. You cannot be separated from your brother, life. You are in IT and your brother is part of yourself and all are part of God.

Rest in peace.

The Wesak festival of power and love and compassion.

Listen

If you could but give yourselves time to withdraw from the outer or material planes of life, and *listen*! When sitting at peace in your garden, or walking in the open places within your towns, or in quiet country lanes, give yourselves time to listen to the voice of love, which will then surely make itself known in the quiet of your soul.

This, beloved brethren, is the great secret of life on the earth plane. Those who live on the material plane only are barren, are starved; whatever work they put their hand to do, if they are not contacting the spirit, or the voice of God, in the quiet of their own souls, they do not dwell in the fullness they were intended to by our Father. He has given unto His children the gift of love, the gift of wisdom, which lies in the heart. Another name for this gift is the spirit of Christ.

Test our words for yourselves; observe those who are trying, according to their own understanding, to express artistic, musical or literary gifts, or the gift of healing, and note how many of these are in touch with that mysterious spiritual *life*. Those so in touch express the life of the spirit in their work; others working purely on the intellectual plane may give brilliant service, brilliant work to the world, but there is something lacking if the spirit does not shine through. In a perfectly executed piece of music—technically perfect —unless the spirit is within, it fails in its purpose. So cultivate the art of listening, in your quiet moments, to the spirit, and it will speak ever in one language, that of love. Love brings to your heart peace, kindliness, tolerance, a desire to forget selfish aims, and a longing to *give* that which your spirit has revealed to you, to the rest of humanity.

The Whitsun Blessing

We want you to think of Whitsun as a time of renewed brotherhood. The brethren met together *with one accord in one place*. This gathering together of men and women in one spirit, with one accord, was part of the religion of the God-men who came to earth in the beginning to help young humanity to find the way of truth, to find the way to God. And how they taught these young souls was to gather them together at certain times (such as the solstices and equinoxes, and at the time of the full moon when a special power comes to the earth) and show them how to raise their consciousness to God, and to receive the inflow of the Christ love into their hearts.

It is no new thing for humanity to meet together in groups or brotherhoods; throughout the ages men and women have drawn together in one spirit to worship the Sun, and to worship the great Mother spirit, the Source of all life and giver of all sustenance. So when the early Christian brothers met together they were only following a pattern which they had learnt from their forefathers: a pattern of meeting together for quiet communion and worship of God, giver of all life; worship of the great Mother, the giver of all sustenance.

For the men of those remote days all nature was their pattern, their picture of God. Man today will have to learn to come into harmony with natural law, and with spiritual law, which is simply the law of love, the law which says 'give love'. Man is so involved with his material life, so involved in all the worries and anxieties of the physical life, that he has no time to withdraw from the world and attune himself to that beautiful cosmic love which would put all things right on your earth. Men think they must fight for their rights. But Jesus did not teach you this. Jesus taught you to be still . . . to love; the elder brethren, the great masters of all time and all ages, have all taught the same fundamental truth. This does not mean that you do nothing to heal a wound, or to heal the wounds of your fellow men; it means that you practise the law of brotherhood, and by so doing set in motion the power of divine magic which can overcome all darkness.

Whatever the conflict, whatever the problem in your life, if you will be patient and give love, give thanks, give forth the spirit of Christ the Son, you will find that the magic will work. Divine magic is the power of brotherhood, the power of the star, the power of the Christ love, which will make all crooked places straight. This is a very positive state of mind, a state of positive good by which you help the whole world.

And so at Whitsuntide the brethren drew together in one accord, in love. They raised their consciousness to the heavenly life, to the light; and as they waited, and the light poured down into their hearts, they were filled, filled with the spirit. The Great White Brotherhood consists of the souls of men and women who have consciously received this outpouring from the Son of God, from the Great White Light.

IV

The Summer Festival

Concerning the Spiritual Sun

LET US consider the meaning of the sun. The sun gives to you life and warmth, but it also gives to you spirit—so said the Ancient Wisdom. For the ancient belief is that behind the physical sun which you see in the heavens is the spiritual radiation, the spiritual life-force which feeds and sustains all life on earth.

It is this spiritual counterpart of the sun which we in the spirit world worship as the Cosmic Christ. But the Cosmic Christ is not only a radiation, a power unseen and too often unfelt: it has form, a human form. We do not say that the whole radiation of the spiritual emanation from the Sun can be confined to one human form; we say that it can manifest in great power through a perfectly beautiful human form.

Is not this comforting to learn, that God the Father caused this divine Sunlight to take human form, for the Sun—or Son—in human form creates a bridge between man and his Creator. Some people say that they can go direct to God, which is true; but if you were bereft of your friends on earth you would be very lonely indeed. If you were the only man or woman on these islands, how lonely you would feel, and you would have some difficulty in understanding the love of God. But if you are companioned by someone similar to yourself, someone who has a human smile, who can speak to you your own human language, who can fold you to his heart—what a difference it makes to your loneliness! God knows this, and that is why these wonderful manifestations such as Jesus Christ, Krishna, the Buddha—all of the Sun spirit, come to humanity.

We would like you to conceive the perfect human form of the Cosmic Christ, or Christ the lord of earth's humanity, surrounded by His younger brethren who are part of His spirit, all part of the spirit of the whole—all brethren of the same spirit. In this manner His life is being spent for earth's humanity.

It is for you to seek this divine Presence, to become attuned to it, to become at one with it; and then you will know that you too are all truly brethren, all of the same spirit.

We have tried in these bare words to open your consciousness to this beloved and tender form of perfect man through whom pours the splendour of the spiritual Sun upon you, loving and knowing and uplifting you always.

Spiritual Unfoldment should bring human Strength

We cannot do more than tell you what a wonderful life awaits you. It can be experienced by you who are in the body, now at this very present time, but it will certainly be in the future when you have claimed your sonship, and the gifts which God has implanted in your heart.

We often notice in our earthly brethren a weariness of soul, and body in some cases, and this should not be. You must understand that the source of all physical health, happiness and harmony is the one great Light; but you allow yourselves to get into a state of confusion. It is so easy to forget the power all around you and within you. Instead of the line that connects you with your soul body and your real self being thick and strong, it becomes weak. Your body becomes depleted and you get tired and full of fears. Dear children, banish fear. What is there to fear? —nothing. Usually the great enemy of man is death. Most men fear death, but death is the Angel sent by the Father to draw the unwilling bolts and to set the soul free, like a bird. If you are not afraid of death are you afraid of loneliness? You are never alone. All those you love are very close, indeed, they are one with you, part of you. They understand your thoughts, and their love for you is greater than ever it was on earth. Are you afraid of poverty, of being without the necessities of life? Who feeds you and clothes you, my brothers?—the Great White Spirit. He will never fail you but you must attune yourself to His life. You must surrender yourselves to His love and His wisdom, for He knows your needs, my children, and will never fail in His supply. You cut yourselves off from His supply by forgetting that He is the source of all supply on every plane of your being, spiritual, mental, physical.

We understand the vicissitudes and the difficulties of your life. We want you to know something beyond the personal, we want you to keep hold of that real spiritual power which will bring into your life all the sunshine of the Beloved—all the peace and happiness that you feel has escaped you. Seek the Source and do not dwell too much on the limitations of the physical and material life. Brothers, rise above them and then you will feel this spiritual power flowing through you, and will know that you have found the jewel of great price. No one can rob you of that jewel. It is God's gift. Seek ye first the kingdom of God, and you will have all that you need on every plane of your being. Do not fret if you do not get it at once. It does not matter. It is coming to you; be patient and rest in God.

The Christ Festival

You come from the Sun, the source of light and happiness for all humanity, love; and to the Sun you all return, but in full consciousness of the powers which your Father–Mother God gave you at your birth from the great Heart, the cosmic Heart, the centre of love, wisdom and power.

The message of Jesus, the Christ, is the message of eternal life. Understand that life itself is the Sun in you, and the Sun is the Christ spirit; and that the

Christ spirit is divine love, which is ever creative, ever bringing light out of darkness.

The greatest work you can do on your earth is to turn your faces to the light, to live for the light and to help all men towards this realisation of light. You are not born to live in darkness and unhappiness and hardship. You are born so that you may develop the powers of the Sun in your soul; and unless man is doing this he is not making use of his life as God intended.

At the full moon when the sun is in the sign of Gemini there is a great festival in the heavens, the Christ festival, when there is an exceptional spiritual outpouring upon the earth and into the hearts of men from the Christ Sun. The ceremony takes place on the plane of what we call the white ether. The white ether is the level of consciousness where all souls can hold communion with the Son of God, the Cosmic Christ. It is the plane of reunion, the plane of true brotherhood; it is the plane of the Cosmic Christ. At this level the great Christ festival takes place, and those who are functioning always at the Christ level look to their brothers in the flesh to be channels through whom they can pour the light and love of the Christ Sun on to earth's humanity.

And so, at the time of the full moon in June and near the summer solstice, give yourself time to withdraw, mentally, from the cares and attractions of the physical life and, in spirit, join the company of those assembled high in the etheric peaks of life, on that plane of the white ether. Be very still in mind and body, try to feel that point of light in your heart which is of the Sun, and receive into your heart the glorious outpouring from the heart of the Sun . . . and become an instrument to radiate light and love to all mankind.

The Fragrance of the Rose

Centre your thoughts and your feelings upon the symbol of the Christ love, the sweet rose. Contemplate its fragrance and the beauty of its form and imagine that your heart is a rose and that its fragrance permeates your being. This is the emblem of the life of a brother or a sister . . . fragrant and pure, still and patient, permeating the surroundings of the life with the light and beauty and fragrance of Christ.

Brethren, the greatest work is done through love, only love. You can all feel the beauty of spiritual love. Human love is very sweet, it is very dear to the human heart; but as it widens, as it rises onto the plane of spirit, it widens and becomes universal. There is nothing sweeter or more powerful than love. Love may find expression in material gifts, in acts of service, but love never loses its power to create good. The more you can feel love, the one towards the other, and give forth love into the world, the more you are raising the whole vibration of the earth. You know your life is transformed when you are able to

48

maintain a feeling of love. It is true that love is the saviour of mankind . . . love, the saviour of the world. Therefore let us continue to love and to be lovely in the sight of our Father–Mother God.

June is the month of roses, the symbol of love. The symbol of our Master is the rose; the rose which pours forth perfume, which inspires everyone with happiness and joy and love. It is the month of the Lord Christ, the Son of God.

May love bloom like the rose in the garden of the temple of your heart.

V

Harvest

Natural Food

IF DURING the summertime of harvest you look round at the beautiful gifts of Mother Earth, you will realise that they could not be there without the touch of God. Some people will say, 'This is just the natural law, the automatic outworking of nature.' No, these things are not done by nature alone but by the power of a divine Intelligence. The great Mother Earth plays her part. The Sun of God gives life and sheds light and warmth and produces the rain, to water the earth; and man plays his part, for God uses man to prepare the earth and to sow the seeds. And then from a small seed or tuber, there is produced a miracle of beauty, and food for you—food for the physical body and food for the mind; and for the spirit too, for do not forget that the physical food you take into your body affects not only the cells of the physical body but the subtler bodies too. We would like you to realise this. In this new age of Aquarius there will be a special outpouring of blessing upon humanity, but unless men are ready, purified, so that their vehicles become sensitive to the outpoured spirit, they will not receive the blessing into themselves in the same degree. There is a need in this new age of Aquarius for the bodies of man to be purified by the food of nature: sun-kissed food, wheat, fruits, nuts, vegetables, all the sweet, pure products of Mother Earth. Shall we say, of Mother Earth, the Father God and Christ the Son? As these natural pure foods are taken into the body, so the body increases in its sensitivity to spiritual things, the brain becomes a little more active and more receptive to the inspiration which flows to man from higher and more evolved beings. Now do not be unwise, only take one step at a time. We are just pointing out to you the trend of things in the new age and it will not be many years before this idea which is being broadcast from our world will take root everywhere. We assure you that more sensible and purer food is a spiritual necessity, and it will in time have an effect upon all men's natures. It is necessary for the purification of the body, before the outpouring of the spirit which has been promised in the new age.

Nourishment for Plants

We foresee a time when man will not consume animal flesh; he will not consume any substance which has at some time been individually conscious. Now let us consider the plant kingdom: it is sometimes used as an argument against the practice of vegetarianism that the vegetables you eat have life too. They do have life—that is, the life-force pulses in them; but they have not achieved individual con-

51

sciousness; and while man is in a physical body he has to take into that physical body certain life-forces which, until he reaches a much higher level of evolution still, he can only receive through growing matter; matter which contains this living force. Now, that very life-force in vegetables, in the fruits of the earth, is enhanced or increased by the light, not only the normal physical sunlight, but also the spiritual sunlight. This is why love and tender care of a plant or the earth gives to the growing thing genuine and effective nourishment.

The white light, or love, nourishes the growing thing.

Harvest and the Great Mother

Harvest thanksgiving is not a modern festival, but has been celebrated throughout the ages. We have memories of equinoctial ceremonies when the harvest was gathered in, and our people gave thanks to the Great White Spirit for life itself—for each harvest actually meant another lease of life to the people in those days. We were taught to look upon the earth as the Great Mother. We would help you in your modern world to increase your awareness of the Great Mother who gives so abundantly of her fruits, her grain; of her flowers and her healing herbs. She gives to mankind sustenance: but also her comfort, her healing and all the blessings of man's physical life. You have reason to thank the Great Mother for all these gifts. Let us also include in our thankfulness all the angels of nature who work with her.

The brotherhoods of old, as many of you know, worshipped and loved nature, and endeavoured to live in harmony with the entire family of nature. We are thinking of the period of life of which we have spoken when we ourselves lived as an American Indian of the South. We worked in harmony with the laws of nature. We would sow our corn directed by the invisible brotherhood, using a ritual unknown to man at the present time to call on the invisible forces to stimulate the seed in the soil and to feed our crops; and also a powerful ritual to call down the rain, or bring the sunlight to warm the grain. People should learn once again to live in tune with natural forces, should be sowing, growing, blessing their food by power of the love of the Great White Spirit within their hearts. We, in the past, learned in this way how to direct the invisible and spiritual forces and thus work in co-operation with Mother Earth and the Great White Spirit, the heavenly Father.

Man at present is concerned chiefly with physical science; he wants to find out about physical conditions beyond the earth. He wants to know about life in outer space. But he must not overlook the more important spiritual science he needs for the development of his spiritual body. He must recognise that he lives in a world of radiation; and that around his physical plane are many radiations of super-physical life, radiations of goodness, of wisdom and knowledge. Above all, he is encompassed by the love of invisible worlds. When he is humble enough to recognise that all around him is the power, the life-force he needs for his growth and development, physically, mentally and spiritually, then he will tap in to forces at present unknown. Man shares in a community of life invisible as well as visible.

From a Talk on a Summer Evening: the Fairy and Angelic Kingdoms

A wonderful world exists at the etheric level—what you would call a fairy world, an angelic kingdom—and all the spirits of the elements, of the wind and the water, and the sunshine and the earth. All these so-called fairy and angelic beings are as real as you are and have beautiful bodies built of white ether.

These 'fairy folk' have a great part to play in the development of man's life on earth. For instance, the fairy folk, under the direction of the earthly Mother and her angels, are responsible for the production of sustenance for your physical body. We look forward to a time when greater co-operation comes between these peoples of the higher ethers and man on earth. When man becomes sufficiently open to these higher influences and is consciously developing his solar body, or the body of the sun, he will no longer have any appetite for the flesh of animals but will have a greater desire to eat the fruits of the earth.

There are other spirits of the earth, the gnomes,

who are concerned with the very substance of the earth, with its jewels and stones. Then there are the sylphs of the air who carry the air currents and bring you the air you breathe, and the winds which blow good to you as well as taking away darkness and evil. Remember also the spirits of the water and of the fire, the salamanders and those great beings the sun spirits, who work under the great solar lords. These etheric beings are as necessary to man as he is to them in the scheme of creation, and in the evolution of life in etheric and physical matter.

We have spoken often before of ceremonies with which we were very familiar in our American Indian days, when the people joined in grand ceremonies of planting the seeds and bringing down the Great White Light into the earth to stimulate their growth. We called upon the angels of the water to bring the rain, the angels of the sun to give warmth to the seeds which we had planted. Our people in those days were all working together with the etheric kingdoms. But now, unfortunately, it is all machinery! Man must get back to the real, the true, the God way of life, of working together with the angelic and etheric kingdoms. His life on earth will become richer and he will begin to see that all is eternal life. Earth herself demonstrates this to you now, but you do not recognise it; for are not the seasons which bring forth the flower and fruit, and harvest that provides all you need for your sustenance, the expression of this eternal life? And behind all nature are the beloved etheric brethren who work in the soil and with all growing things, and bring forth the food which gives you life and health.

Remember too that you can give a great deal of help to the etheric workers, to those who work with the plants for man's sustenance; you can be responsive to the angels of the air who inspire man in the creative arts, and in all works of creation. Most of all you can help by your God thought and by your love. All this creation at the etheric level of life is very receptive to the quality of man's thought, and this is why the brotherhood is now endeavouring to instil good, brotherly thought into men's minds.

God be with you all. God is with you and the angels smile upon you. See with your higher mind the waving golden cornfields. See God's food and the food from the earthly Mother providing for her children. O Lord, we thank Thee for Thy blessing.

A Law of Giving and Receiving

A divine law operates through both the act of giving and the act of receiving. Experience has taught you that by creating a condition of love and harmony deep within your own heart you draw to yourself love and harmony; by creating beauty within, you draw external beauty to you. In other words, as you give, so you receive. What you put into life flows back in full measure—this is inescapable law. It is impossible for any man or woman to give truly from the heart without receiving exactly what they have given—and a great deal more if the heart is attuned to the Master of love.

The working of this law is very clearly recognised when the soul withdraws from the physical body and awakens in the spirit world, for then it finds itself in the very conditions it has built for itself through its thoughts and actions while on earth. It receives as it has given. There is no escaping the result of our actions, and as we sincerely serve our brother man so we serve ourselves. If we hurt any one of God's creatures we ourselves suffer that same hurt. Again— as we give so shall we receive.

Again, Jesus said, *Lo, I am with you alway*. May we suggest the inner meaning of these words to you? The law of Christ Jesus is that you love one another; and *if* you love your brother man, *Lo, I am with you alway, even unto the end of the world*. By loving and by obeying the commands of the great Spirit of love you are asking for and receiving the eternal presence of the Master. You set in motion those spiritual forces which attune your consciousness to the Source of all being, and into your innermost you receive streams of light and power from the Lord Christ, the saviour of all mankind, who is all love and light. As His light flows into your heart, you are raised out of the bondage of fear, sickness and death, into the radiance of the spirit life.

Those who love, those who serve from the heart, reap what they sow, and the eternal presence of

57

Christ, the Master of love, walks the earth with them. *Lo, I am with you alway.*

But yet another truth is contained in the injunction: *Ask, and it shall be given you*, for every soul needs to know the Source of its help, and every soul must learn how to approach its Master, and ask for the spirit of love, understanding and wisdom. But before the soul can truly ask it has first to become simple and pure in heart, stripped of all pride, arrogance and self-justification, and without fear. Stripped of all that hinders its approach to its Master, the soul asks, it seeks, it knocks at the door. Then the door is opened. That which was sought is found.

Those who live by the divine law of love and harmony, holding before them always the vision of the Master, those who practise the divine law of giving and receiving, develop rich gifts of the spirit; and all they need, physically, mentally and spiritually, is added unto them. In other words they ask in the spirit of the little child, in purity and simplicity and love, and God hears the petition and pours down upon His child all that it needs on every plane of being. With deep earnestness we are telling you the secret of happiness as we have seen it revealed on the higher planes of life.

Patience

When a sower sows his seed he has to entrust that seed to God. He has to resign his seed to the care of

Mother Earth, to the great Master. He must not disturb it, resting confident that the wonder of growth will take place. To those of you who find life sometimes tiresome because things won't work out quickly enough for you, we say try to remember not to keep on pulling up your seeds to see what is happening. Be patient—as the sower has to be. He has to have confidence in the powers that be; and the growth of the seed comes to pass.

Man is never satisfied. He wants everything exactly right, to be not too hot, not too cold, not too wet, not too dry. He wants everything all his own way, but what does he himself do to produce that perfect balance? That is the question. When man can once learn to find a balance within himself, to bring about the balance between his spiritual and his physical life; when he creates the right conditions out of his own soul, then he will have everything exactly as he wants it!

The Love that guides Man's Journey

Some of you find it so difficult to believe that your Creator is all love. But when you are able to see the whole journey of your spirit from the moment of its sowing to the time of its reaping, and understand how a perfect justice, love and mercy has operated throughout, you will indeed prostrate yourselves in thanksgiving before the perfection of the law which is ever at work in all man's sowing and reaping. As man sows today he will reap tomorrow—that is the law which rules the countless incarnations of man. But may we add this—that whilst man himself may, through his materialistic outlook, be a harsh judge of his brother man, God, Who is all love, looks down on His children with compassion and mercy, ever giving His children opportunities to respond to the outpouring of love from the heavenly hosts.

Oh, my children, if only we could persuade you to hold fast to faith, to trust in your Creator! If we could only persuade you at all times to enter the silence when you are troubled, and then with patience and courage say, and mean: 'Not my will but Thy will, O Lord, be done!' In those silent moments you invoke the power of God. Be still then, and know that God is love.

The Bread and the Wine

At the present time men and women are feeling a stimulation in their etheric bodies, in what you call the psychic centres or chakras. The ordinary person does not quite understand what is happening but finds himself dissatisfied with the old order and searching for new truth. On every hand men and women are searching, longing for comfort, for knowledge, for peace. The soul of man is hungry, and cries to its Creator for bread and wine. Throughout the ages man has partaken of the bread and wine, has been renewed in spirit through the holy sacrament (or as it was sometimes called in ancient days, the feast of remembrance). Nevertheless through his own desire and choice, and also through his own self-seeking man has latterly had to pass through a cycle of darkness, where he has been unable to eat the bread or drink the wine of true life. His prayer is now being answered, for the living bread and wine is coming in abundance to humanity, and true religion is coming back into the heart and life of man.

One of the first ceremonies which men and women who have entered upon the path must share and fully comprehend, is the ceremony of the sacrament, or feast of remembrance. In days to come the wise man will be ready to learn, to appreciate the importance of ceremonial and ritual, and understand the invisible activity behind religious practices. We do not mean that you must go back to outworn ceremonies from which the spirit and the life has gone, but that you will come to understand the purpose of new ceremonies and new rituals in your religious life and in your daily life, which are to stimulate men's higher bodies so that they come into realisation of their true being.

The feast of remembrance, under whatever name, was always celebrated in the temples of the past. The bread and wine laid upon the altar represented the gifts of Mother Earth to her human family. Through partaking of these gifts, in the right spirit, the people were raised in consciousness. As they took part in this feast of remembrance, remembering the Source of all bounty, they lost that personal arrogance which

61

today dulls so many earthly people to the realities of the spirit. They realised that all that they had, and all that they were which was noble and beautiful, came from the same Source, the Father–Mother God, the spiritual Sun shining in the heavens. They took the bread and the wine in remembrance of the Source of all life and the communion they shared with all life. The bread, the corn that feeds the body of man, is the body of the Sun (not only the physical sun but the spiritual Sun behind the outer manifestation), because the Sun interpenetrates the particles of the earth to bring forth the corn. The fruits of the earth, the corn and the grapes, are the substance of the Sun, from which all derive life. Sunlight and rain, earth and air have nurtured them. Therefore, my friends, every mouthful we eat should be a remembrance. Every meal taken should be a divine communion. With every fragment of food which passes the lips one should say, 'This is the divine body, this is the substance of God. This comes to me through the divine love; therefore I eat in remembrance of God. I eat the bread of life, I drink the wine of life.'

Yet there is also the esoteric interpretation of this divine communion. The bread is symbolic also of the sustenance from God necessary to the human spirit. Think of the bread and wine as symbols of human experience; and when you are told to receive, and eat the bread, understand that it means that you accept the karma of your life, knowing that it is indeed your food. Your experience is the food which helps the soul and spirit to grow towards perfect manhood and womanhood, towards man made perfect. The wine is the juice of the grapes passed through the winepress. This again is the symbol of human experience: how man himself has to be squeezed and suffers either physically or emotionally; but out of suffering is produced the most beautiful, sweet, divine essence, the essence of divine love. This essence or wine strengthens the soul, heals the wounds made by the difficulties and the disappointments of life. The disciple accepts the bread and wine of life's experience with thankfulness.

When men and women partake of true communion, the Christ in them reaches out to enfold all creation; reaches up and is absorbed into the very heart of God.

VI

The Autumn Equinox

From a Talk on an Autumn Evening:
an American Indian Memory

DEAR brethren, we would like you to come with us on a journey! Close your eyes, close your senses to the outer world, and imagine that we are all sitting around a camp fire under a starlit sky with the brotherhood of nature. The scene we depict is in fact quite familiar to many of you, and it will not be very difficult for you to go back in memory to the times when we all assembled in a large circle, sitting upon Mother Earth watching the camp fire burning in our midst, smelling the perfumes of the earth and the pines and the flowers and the woods; looking up to the canopy of heaven, gazing upon the twinkling stars. These were more to the Indian brothers than little lights in the sky, for they represented those powers of God which can destroy and recreate. We learnt to accept all that God sent to us as being good, for we understood that the Great White Spirit, all love and wisdom, was in supreme command; we knew that the great planetary beings and angels, right down to our nature spirits, all obeyed the command of the Great White Spirit.

Picture, then, all the brethren gathered in the hush of the evening, listening to the orchestra of nature—the wind in the pines, the murmur of the insects and faint twitter of birds and little cries of furry beasts, beaver and rat and all the tiny creatures of the water and woods—all one great happy brotherhood, living under the protection and by the love of the invisible power, the Great White Spirit. Even as we gazed up into the heavens, to the stars, they spoke to our innermost heart of love, of brotherhood, of peace. . . .

In this present cycle and in your generation, you are so clothed with civilisation that you are shut away from this contact, through nature, with the Great White Spirit; and because you are cut off from the direct contact with nature you suffer from nerve strain, which sometimes develops into disease; you suffer from all kinds of strange diseases which even your brilliant medical men and women are unable to define. And still the soul longs for this unknown comfort and strength from the Source of life. You endeavour to contact this glorious Spirit through your mind, but in the old days we tapped it directly through our senses. Mankind has again to learn the use of his five senses, for through the five senses (which are allied to vortices of power in the etheric body) can be drawn wonderful spiritual power and life-force.

Through imagination then, through using the sense of smell, the sense of touch, the sense of hearing, of taste and sight on the etheric plane, let us contact nature here, around our camp fire.

We are endeavouring to awaken in each one of you an awareness of the vast brotherhood of life. Seated in a circle around our fire we feel in our innermost being a living peace, and true brotherhood and unity. Let us radiate this peace, a creative power, into the ether, that it may find a resting place in the deep subconscious mind of humanity. . . .

Do you see? Oh, we beg you to see, the small furry creatures, the beaver, the rats with bright eyes, dormice, frogs, and the little creatures of the earth— see them all around us, all joining in with our brotherhood; even owls and sleepy birds, all one. Even the crackle of the fire is causing the salamanders to leap about, and nearby at the river we can hear the splash of the water sprites; we hear the wind in the trees, and the spirits of the air are winging their way to join our brotherhood. Peace on earth . . . goodwill to all life.

Live and rest in this consciousness, my dear ones. Don't rush and tear about and get anxious over things which do not matter. Be at peace, radiate peace . . . quietly perform your tasks, keeping always within your heart the memory of the true life which is yours.

A Soul Lesson for the Autumn Equinox, when the Sun is in Libra

We in spirit rejoice in the brotherhood of service with our earthly brethren. We thank God our Father and Mother for our brotherhood, and in thanking God for the brotherhood that we know, let us learn to thank God for the universal brotherhood which is ours, although we do not yet fully recognise it. We ask that each morning you will give a thought to the brotherhood of life, and thank God for this brotherhood, for the kindliness of humanity. May we all cultivate a sense of humour, so that we see as amusing those things in humanity which would irritate and annoy. Let us be understanding, feeling with our brother in his little irritations and annoyances, and turn darkness into light by throwing upon it the warming beam of humour. But in humour it is necessary to be wise. Let it not be unkindly, but kindly humour.

There are certain times on the earth plane when humanity is affected by what you would call difficult planetary influences. It is not easy to be placid and happy. Little things are very trying. But the wise man rules his stars, and is not ruled by them; and by aspiring to the light of the Perfect One, man can overcome the influences of the planets which are affecting his life—affecting it not with a view to upsetting it, or causing sorrow, but affecting it to teach and strengthen the soul. To the best of your ability, respond to the light of brotherhood, kindliness, humour and good temper; we know of no better way of climbing the path which leads to the grand temple in the heavens.

St Michael and All Angels

On September 29th you celebrate the festival of St Michael and All Angels. The archangel Michael is one of the Sun spirits, a messenger from the Sun, the sphere of the Cosmic Christ; and the sword he wields is that of spiritual truth, which Christ places in the hand of every one of his followers—the truth of the spirit or of the Son of God indwelling within every human breast. This is the weapon which will guard man through every crisis of his human life, which will give him strength to overcome.

At the beginning of this new age of brotherhood, the Age of Aquarius, with its vast potentialities for destruction as well as progress, it is necessary for all peoples who understand the power of the light to work with the angels of the light, to give their allegiance to the archangel Michael and all his angels, so that the white light may maintain the equilibrium and bring mankind into that golden age which is waiting to manifest on earth.

It is a time when angels from heaven are drawing very close, breaking through the barriers of darkness and unbelief, and bringing the light to men. We want you all to become familiar with this companionship, and believe that angels can help you in many, many ways. All people are guided, throughout their days on earth by an angelic guardian. When you are sad think of the radiant angels who are very near to you. Give them your confidence, having yourself done your very best. Then be ready to respond and they will lead you out of your prison into the freedom of the spirit.

Have no fear, my children. Attune yourselves to this invisible company of angels, and you will find their power manifests in your daily life.

St Francis' Day

We would speak of Brother Francis, who draws very close at this season of the year to stimulate compassion in men's hearts—compassion towards your little brethren of the air, the sea and the earth.

You know, my children, when we were in the body of flesh, a long time ago now, we learnt from our elder brethren never wantonly to slay any creature of the animal kingdom. In the particular incarnation of which we speak, we were taught never to torture or slay for sport or to abuse our little brethren in any way.

Then, the conditions of life were such that sometimes there was nothing else to sustain the physical body except animal flesh, but this is not so today. There are plenty of grain foods, and fruits and vegetables, seeds and nuts—the earth abounds in vitalising foods which can give man all he needs for the sustenance of his physical body. We want you to remember this and to think with compassion of all your brethren in the animal kingdom, and of the suffering inflicted on them, not least at the time of the Christmas festival. We ask you to do all you can to alleviate this suffering on your earth plane, for we say most earnestly that until man himself refrains from cruelty to the brethren of the animal kingdom, and to Mother Earth, as well as to the human kingdom, man himself will suffer. His physical body is now becoming more sensitive and will absorb the vibrations of the cruelty so rampant on earth today.

Man himself must be the first to respond to the rays coming from the higher world, and to radiate those rays of love. . . .

A Thought for Autumn

Know that from the darkness of the earth life, there springs and flourishes that which flowers in beauty, giving forth perfume and radiance. When you plant a bulb in the autumn you have faith that from that brown globe will spring a creation so charged with beauty as to seem a veritable breath of God. It will rise from the depths of darkness, though rooted in decay.

This it is, beloved child, that the masters see coming to glorify God's earth—a human life of beauty, breathing the essence of the God life.

And so we say that whatever may be your circumstances or your troubles at this present time, be thankful; for they are the soil about your roots, from which the blossoms will spring forth in due season.

VII

The Festivals of All Souls and of Remembrance

AUTUMN

After the culmination, in the harvest thanksgiving, of all the vigorous growth and activity of the summer season, it is good to feel the gentle peace of autumn pervading the fields and woodlands, parks and gardens, even the very earth herself. As the sap withdraws into the roots and the life-force within the earth becomes for a time quiescent, this deepening peace becomes almost tangible. This is a time of the balancing of the life-forces. The eternal law of balance manifests in every aspect of life, in light and darkness, summer and winter, the ebb and flow of the tides, and in so many ways in the wonderful mechanism of the human body. It manifests too in the swinging of the human consciousness between the outer and the inner worlds, between waking and sleeping, life and death. The coming of autumn in the northern hemisphere is the beginning of spring in the southern hemisphere, and vice versa. So too, the withdrawal of human life from physical manifestations means birth on the inner plane. We mourn the death of the body but those on the other side of life rejoice because the soul is born again to them. In nature the withdrawal of life from outward form is quiet; but even as the leaves fall and the golden stubble is ploughed in and the quiet of autumn settles upon the land, deep

72

below the outward manifestation a new life is stirring, as it were a heavenly spring-time.

The festivals which fall at this time, the ancient festival of Hallowe'en, the festival of All Souls and All Saints, and also the more modern festival of Remembrance, are a reminder that deep within every soul lies the power to commune with heavenly beings and with this inner world of spirit. At this time of the year our thoughts turn inward to the world of spirit, to those who dwell therein, and the two worlds are very close; and, as if to balance the loss of physical sunlight there comes a special outpouring of spiritual light onto the earth plane, which, in those who can attune themselves to it, helps to strengthen their conscious contact with the spiritual Sun, the Source of all life. In this union with God comes also the comfort of true communion with loved ones who have withdrawn from the body of flesh. The time is essentially one of communion with the world of spirit.

At the Time of All Souls

WE PRAY that your inner vision may open to the company of shining ones, friends and brothers of your spirit, who draw close to you at the festival of All Souls.

We cannot give you any physical proof of our message of the eternal life, but God has given you the power within your heart to receive your own confirmation of its truth. You may search the world over. You may use every scientific instrument man can devise, you can seek through the ways of psychic

73

phenomena—yet still this great truth of eternal life evades man when he searches only along the earthly path. There is always something beyond all earthly things, something elusive which cannot be caught, trapped and harnessed by the mind of man. It is so free, so subtle, that it can only be realised in man's own heart. Man has been given the gift of God in him; within man's own being is the life of God, and it is his work here on earth so to live as to stimulate the growth of this God-consciousness.

How can we describe the invisible worlds? How can we convey to you their beauty? Will it help you to understand how to register the impression of this higher world when we tell you to seek God through beauty and love? Seek awareness through love for all creation, through love for your fellow man, through love for your life, and through love for God Himself. Seek it through the joy which can be found in very simple things. If you will do this, you will begin to become aware of a subtle presence—yes, like the perfume of a rose, but also the perfume of the wide earth, the sea, the air; a subtle all-pervasive perfume which will speak to you of the presence of loved ones. You will begin to become aware of a life which is eternal; you will know when an angel passes, for you will be developing that higher sense of the spiritual life, the life of the realms of light to which your loved ones pass when the body dies.

Death of the body should not cut you off from them; only *you* really cut yourself off from them. For these worlds of light, although they are real and solid to those who live in them, are *inner* worlds. This may be difficult for you to understand. In order to reach this world you must turn inwards, to the innermost sanctuary of the spirit, and there worship God in humility and with a gentle loving spirit.

Jesus, who was the channel for the Christ light, for the spirit of the Son of God, said: *Seek ye first the king-dom of God . . . and all these things shall be added unto you.* This is the bridge, my children. If you seek the inner worlds by the way of the spirit of Christ, the veil of the temple will be torn asunder, and you will be able to approach the holy of holies. This means that deep in the centre of your being an awareness of the one-ness of all life will come to you. This will bring you true communion, spirit with spirit, and you will be filled with joy. You may receive what you call proof by other means, but after a while it will fade, and you will remain unsatisfied until you have found this pearl of great price within your own being. Then you will be satisfied.

From a Talk at a Remembrance Service

We come from the realms of spirit to greet you with love; and on this special occasion of Remembrance we would remember all the men and women who have selflessly served their brother man. We have a special reason tonight to give thanks for the courage in the human heart; and to praise God, the Great

75

White Spirit, for this courage given to the human soul in times of need. We who look down from the spirit life are particularly impressed by the courage we see in countless human hearts.

This we emphasise on the night of Remembrance, and we commend to you all the importance and the wonder of the courage which has been implanted in man by his Creator. It is true that not all souls have yet developed this quality, but in the end all souls must find courage within themselves. Therefore, to those of you who are engaged in service to mankind, and perhaps find the path very difficult, and your heart failing sometimes through lack of courage, we would say, look up, dear brethren, look up to the Source of all courage. Be not weary in spirit, or disheartened by what you see on the surface in the outer world, in the worldly world.

Even those of you who have touched the heights and seen the vision glorious, who have heard the voice of the spirit, even you may at times feel downcast when you contrast what you see on earth with the life of the spirit. To you especially we say, look up! Pray for courage, and you will not be disappointed; for as you pray, so those who are commissioned by the Great White Spirit to help you will be able to draw very close, and bring you this special gift.

At this moment we ask you to withdraw from that worrying little earthly mind, which is so analytical; put it on one side, open your heart with love and welcome to the heavenly hosts. We would bring you spiritual power to help take the blindfold from your eyes, and show you the concourse of shining souls who are able to draw particularly close to such services as this. Where the brotherhood of the light find sensitive channels through which they can pour the light, they always draw close. Though they are behind the veil created by the material mind and the darkness of depression and disbelief, yet they are very, very close to you. We can see them now, a great assembly of shining souls who have passed through the school of earth and by their service and sacrifice have won release. They know the joy of living and giving to their companions. They come back to you now in this service of Remembrance.

Will it sound too unusual to say they bring their message of *eternal life*? So few of you understand what is meant by eternal life. Some of you may even say, 'I don't *want* to live eternally! I am tired, I would like to go to sleep and forget it all.' Oh, dear, dear ones, if you really feel like that you are shutting the door on a very great and beautiful truth, and a wonderful life which lies before you—and before every human soul who wills to tread that path—not only in the spirit world, but here and now. Material thinking blocks the vision of man; but when a spiritual quickening comes and you can catch a glimpse of the meaning of eternal life, you will no longer feel weary and hopeless.

There is no death. Of what are you afraid? You may look upon an empty shell—like the shell of a chrysalis—and say, 'This is death'. No. Life continues. Life always is, always has been, and always will be. We, who are fully conscious of having passed the great initiation called death, come to you having crossed the bridge of love, a bridge partly created by the love which you have given. God the great spirit has so created you and your bodies—your physical and your higher bodies—that you have the power within you to commune with those you love in the world of spirit. You have material available for the construction of this bridge between the world and the higher ethers. We come to you, and you may also learn to come in full consciousness to us. In your earthly life you can be builders, together with your companions of your spirit, of a bridge between your state of life and the higher life. When man has accomplished his task in full consciousness he will know that the angels and saints, the great army of the brothers of the star, are with him to inspire and help him in all his tasks on earth. This does not mean shifting his earthly responsibilities onto the companions of his spirit. It means his putting the divine law into operation first. Some people think they can sit back and let God and His angels do the work. Oh, no! Man is here to learn a series of vital spiritual truths, which only his daily experience can teach him.

*

There is a further message which the company of the shining army wish us to give. This is about your service on earth, and what you are doing, and what more you can do to forward the coming of the golden age on earth.

Some people think that the world is deteriorating, that humanity is deteriorating. They see only confusion, pain and suffering. They cannot see progress, nor yet what evolution is going to bring. Yet each one of you can be in the vanguard of the great stream of light and brotherhood which is coming to the earth.

Whenever you make an effort to express in any form your love for God, the compassion and love you feel for your fellow man, or when you make your effort to be patient and tolerant, and to hold fast to truth, and to the light in your own heart, you are helping to build on earth the glorious New Jerusalem, the city of light described by St John in his Revelation. You are its builders. Only through man, or *God in man*, can this building of the New Jerusalem come about. You don't have to wait until you go to heaven. You start right now, right here, to live, to think, to speak love, and to accept the law of evolution, of growth, of brotherhood.

Try, my dear ones, to accept this vital truth—that God is in you, and will use you to spread truth and knowledge through love. Never forget the real purpose of your life.

*

And now before we cease speaking to you in this way let us remember together those who have served us, in the course of our earthly lifetime; served in many ways by their love, their care, their effort for our well-being, and particularly those who made the great sacrifice of their life for their brother. We remember and we send our great love and thanksgiving to these companions of our earthly life. Join with us in silent communion.

The peace of God shines in your heart, it remains with you for evermore. The brotherhood are saying to you that this is your work, to radiate this love, this understanding and peace to all men. The heavens open and the petals of the golden rose descend upon you all. The golden rose, not petals of blood but petals of life—the life of the spirit, the Christ spirit—descend upon you now. Their gift to you, the spirit of universal love.

And upon you depends the future. Build, my brethren, build with the substance of the Christ love in your heart. Build the new age of brotherhood and lasting peace. So may it be, brethren.

Life sacrificed in War

Your country and others celebrate Remembrance Day in memory of millions of men and women who sacrificed their lives for what they thought was a just cause. Many people think with great grief of this apparently needless and wanton sacrifice of youthful lives, but we would try to show you another aspect.

Most of you are aware of the governing law of karma operative in human life. You know that nothing happens without cause, that nothing can happen by chance. Men and women, therefore, who lost their lives had a certain path to follow which their karma had created for them. Although they may not have been conscious of it, their souls chose this way of working out their karma. So although you have grieved so deeply over the loss of young lives try to realise that their sacrifice served a deeper and more beautiful purpose than you can yet understand and that, perhaps after a period of purification, they have passed through the mists into a world of beauty, and there found God.

There is another law, the law of compensation, which also operates throughout human life. When you are called upon by the law of karma to endure pain and suffering, remember that this is a discipline which is preparing you to realise and enjoy a richer happiness as a compensation, a happiness you cannot achieve without mastery of the lower nature. You cannot force the gates of heaven. There is an ordered path that every soul must tread. But although you may have to pass through unpleasant conditions, the law of compensation is always at work, for God never takes away without giving something in return. Man should try to recognise the law of compensation which is constantly operating in his daily life.

We are not suggesting that it is right for man to be

called upon to slay his brother. We are only explaining that man has freewill, and chooses thoughts and actions of a nature which may in time produce conditions which cause him to suffer. But God's will is that man should instead learn the way of happiness and love, and so reap joy eternal.

These young souls bereft of their earthly bodies are not disappointed in their hopes, in their careers. Instead, they are given new opportunities which their sacrifice has earned for them. The world of spirit is a real world, as substantial as your own, and its substance of finer ether seems just as solid and real to the spirit people as your matter appears to you. Your loved ones are reclothed in bodies of finer ether, and continue their life, with greater opportunity for developing and expressing their spirit through a higher and purer body.

*

We have often talked about sending out the light, to help those in need. In the spirit world are souls who need light. They are suddenly flung out of life, maybe blown to pieces, or cast violently into the beyond. Such souls as these are instantly and tenderly taken care of. But when they come to themselves; when the etheric body, as if by magic, is very rapidly rebuilt, they may find themselves in a state of confusion or darkness, even loneliness. But not for long—hardly have they realised it before someone is there to help them. In the spirit world are many centres of service, many helpers who are sent out by their 'commanding officer', maybe you would say their master. You would be surprised, my brethren, if you could see the extent of the organisation set up for the help of souls both on the physical plane, and also on the plane immediately beyond, who are in a state of darkness.

Now, every soul is known to one or another of these commanding officers. You think it is incredible, but we assure you it is true. Do you remember Jesus saying that not a sparrow falls on the earth without your Father in heaven, and even the very hairs of your head are all numbered? So it is. From these centres there is sent forth a group (or groups) of ordinary men and women. According to the needs of the particular soul so is the helper chosen, someone who can most easily or readily communicate with the soul in need. If you have at any time had cause to be doubtful or anxious about anyone you love, who either through war or accident has been flung into the spirit world, and wonder what has happened to them, you can remind yourself of these faithful servers, these brethren, who move in groups carrying the light into dark places.

Many, many times a message has come back from a discarnate soul who has said: 'I was caught up in a light', or 'I saw a light; oh, such a blessed light shone in the darkness, and it moved, and I followed'. As they followed they very soon found kind friends waiting to give them exactly what they most needed at that time.

You naturally think of heaven as being a most beautiful place, which indeed it is. Remember at the same time that a comforting meal might seem heavenly to some soul which has just been released from physical conditions. Try to understand that the world of spirit is very natural, very normal, and has all things which the lower etheric of the man—the soul just detached from the physical—still wants, because it still at that stage retains desires of the flesh. All these things are open for it to receive if it wishes.

The Sphere of Reunion

On this special day of Remembrance will you, brethren, also remember the lives of all loved ones (wherever they may be and whoever they are) who are now living in the light of heaven? They are not so remote from you that they cannot know your thoughts, or be aware of your loving feelings for them. This is important; although they are living in a sphere of spiritual light, peace, harmony and beauty, and protected from all dark thoughts of the earth, they are still wide open to your thoughts of love. These thoughts reach them—make no mistake. A scientific law ensures that love goes out to meet love. Love knows no barrier.

*

When you seek contact in the sphere of reunion, attune yourself to the Christ spirit. As you worship, simply create in your mind, by your highest and god-like imagination, a most perfect garden, the most perfect flowers and trees, amidst a rolling landscape. There in the quiet inner garden you will find a white seat. (This white seat has a spiritual significance.) In your highest imagination sit and dwell there communing and praying to God, whose life is visible in every feature of this still garden. As you rest in this garden see and know that your dearest is with you by your side; talk to him or her mentally, and you will receive the contact that you have craved for, not through external means but deep within your own inner being. If only for a flash you will know that life is eternal. You will know too that where there is love there can be no separation; for all souls are part of God, and it is God's law that all souls should meet in communion in spirit. Go half-way to meet them. They will not fail to meet you in God's garden.

This beauty infused into the earthly life of the individual soul must in time raise the level of all life. To this end, we in spirit work without ceasing.

The more Spiritual, the more Human

Do not make the mistake of thinking that when men and women you have loved pass away they become too high and too pure to return. Do not think that because they live in a sphere of light they are cut off from you; that they will go onward without you. We would like to correct that error. We will put it simply.

When love enters the heart, even amongst those in incarnation you will sometimes notice a radiance in the flesh. You may exclaim, 'Oh, what a nice face So-and-so has! How radiant he looks!' His or hers is the radiance of the spirit, of love shining through the physical form. It does not remove that person that he or she is beautified by love. Rather it draws that loved one closer. This same rule applies to those who have passed onward. They are not removed because they are clothed in the radiance of the Sun. On the contrary, the more spiritual a soul becomes the more human it grows, the more understanding of your earthly difficulties. If you could meet the Master face to face, you would find your Master a very dear friend and companion, and not at all like a plaster saint. The illumined souls of men do not condemn their younger brethren; they do not even judge them. They love them. We would have you open your hearts confidently to these radiant friends. Ask in trust for them to come close, and you will feel their companionship, and they will whisper words of love to your heart.

The real purpose of the day of Remembrance is to thin the veil between the earth people and those in the beyond, because the Age of Aquarius is the age in which man's higher consciousness has to be developed and unfolded.

We have often referred to the incident when Jesus told his disciples to follow the man carrying the water pot, which is the symbol of Aquarius, of the

New Age. You too are asked to follow the man of the spirit, so that your higher consciousness may be stimulated and unfolded; and with the progress of each person there slowly spreads all over the earth a state of receptiveness to the message from the spiritual leaders in higher spheres.

VIII

Christmas

The Christmas Festival

THERE is some controversy in your modern world about the historical origin of Jesus Christ. We affirm from the spirit world that Jesus Christ was born in the flesh; surrounded by the great heavenly powers.

There is also another aspect of the story which is universal. This tells of the stimulation of the human heart by power from heaven. At this time of the year a heavenly outpouring of love and wisdom comes from the holy and blessed Trinity, Father–Mother–Son, an outpouring to which all men will respond according to their sensitivity or degree of spiritual evolution. Each aspect of the Godhead has a particular influence on humanity, on man's spirit, his soul, and his body. And at Christmas time in particular the divine Mother (as well as the divine Child) pours forth the love, the joy and the sweetness of the spiritual life. For this reason the heart (or human love) in every one becomes stimulated and there is a desire to think of others, to make contacts which will renew goodwill and kindliness among you all. Never close your heart to this great inflow of light from God at Christmas time.

Following upon this blessing comes the arising of

the physical sun from the depths of what we call winter. When the solstice has passed there is a looking forward to renewal of growth, of life. So the ancients used to celebrate this life-coming, this promise of food, of the fruits of the earth, of sunlight, sunshine, warmth, and all the real joy of living.

The time of preparation, the time of Advent, is beautiful indeed. Every season has its own spiritual significance, but of them all Christmas is the greatest, for it binds the human family together as the heavenly family is bound. The light shines from the heavens and enters the cave, the chakra of the heart. There the light gives life to the Child, renews the Christ life. It is not enough that you accept this truth with your mind. You must accept and believe with your whole being.

O my children, it is life which is coming to you, renewal of life! May you always, always receive this outpouring of the golden life-force from the heavens above! Then you will understand the meaning of the I AM, the God within your heart. Then you will know that the real you, the child of God, is above you in the heavenly world; it is only when you look to that divine Source for all your needs that you will understand the meaning of the Christ mass.

It is the birthday, you say, of Jesus of Nazareth. Yes, that was the historical event. Greater than this, which was a manifestation to the earth people of the love of God, there is also a birth into the heart of humanity, into the soul of humanity, of this universal

89

Christ spirit. Oh, seek, seek and ye shall find, my children! Seek this golden sun. Turn your face to the sun which will be rising again on Christmas Day. Remember that behind that physical sun shines the glory and the power of the eternal, the sun of your universe.

A Mystical Interpretation of the Christ Child

Beloved children, you are drawing near to Christmas, to the time when the Christian world bows its head in worship and adoration to the Son of God. This festival of the Sun (the Son) was carried on by Christianity from what you think of as a pagan faith, the ancient Sun-worship. When the sun was to be born again after the winter solstice the peoples of the ancient races rejoiced at the coming, at the rebirth of the sun. The old sun died, through the cold of the winter, but gave a promise of the rebirth of the sun. This is the origin of the Christ mass, and it is noteworthy that the Christian symbol of the Christ mass is the little child, the new-born son. But this symbol of the child has a spiritual significance for every disciple on the path, the little child in the heart.

Every soul who aspires to the spiritual life must be born again; or, as the Master said, must become as a little child. A child is simple and trusting, has confidence in its parents. The little child of the spirit must be innocent of all ill, pure, lowly, humble, confident, trusting, loving. So each year you have the Christmas festival to teach human hearts the significance of becoming as a little child.

There is nothing greater in life than the Christ light. The Christ light manifests through the human life in the simple ways of a little child. Look at any great one, any one of our elder brethren, or the great masters; and you will see that all manifests with simple sweetness, gentleness, purity and innocence. Being innocent of all ill, they are guileless, they are as children.

Come with us now in spirit, in imagination into the home of the elder brethren, and with us join those beloved souls who, because of the simple spirit of a little child, are shining and radiant with the light of heaven . . . the light which is the power of command and control of the physical and spiritual atoms. This command is not attained by the power of the mind of earth but by the very essence of that lowly spirit of the gentle Christ. This is the spirit of Christmas, the spirit of the pure childlike love, adoration and worship.

The Star

At this time of the year you are celebrating—or we hope you will celebrate from your hearts—the festival of the star. And we would impress you with the significance of this festival, for the four festivals of Christendom are not the possession of the orthodox church, but are cosmic truths, cosmic festivals. This time which you call Christmas is a festival of the most ancient brotherhood this earth knows, and is connected with the star, or the spiritual Sun of life, which is the salvation of humanity. And it lies within each man. This star of brotherhood is the star of sonship, the sonship which we humbly and thankfully claim with our Father–Mother God; and we endeavour to recognise the sonship, the star of the divinity, in every man, regardless of social station, or nationality, colour or creed. All men are stars. Jesus, the great world teacher, came to earth under the pronouncement of the star. It has taken the whole of the Piscean Age, which he ushered in, to bring mankind towards understanding of the meaning of the star. Now as your feet are upon the path of the Aquarian Age, the star is beginning to be known as the symbol of brotherhood, the symbol of the Age of Aquarius, of which the Master Jesus spoke when he directed his disciples to follow the man with the water pot—the man who poured forth the water of the spirit upon the followers of the star, all who are ready to receive.

The Wise Men

When the Wise Men came to Jesus they brought gifts of gold, frankincense and myrrh. The treasure which mystics of all ages seek is the gold within the soul. All true aspirants seek to transmute the base metal within their being into pure gold of the spirit, and the Wise Men bring to you the gold which enables you to transmute the base metal in your souls into pure gold.

They bring you frankincense too, the gift of gentleness and sweetness. This sweet fragrance the wise teachers, the radiant ones, bring to you for you to absorb into your soul.

They bring yet another gift, the gift of myrrh, bitterness—some people call it sorrow and pain. All brethren, at some time, feel pain, and this brings understanding and sympathy; pain is necessary for the soul, so that it may grow spiritually and emotionally. Through what you call sorrow, the soul enters into joy.

These beautiful gifts the Wise Men bring to the Christ child which is born in the cave. In the cave of the heart the Christ child is born, deep, deep within your own soul. And to everyone, when the Christ child awakens, or is born in the heart, there follows the visitation of the Wise Men with their gifts of gold, frankincense and myrrh. Therefore, my children, we welcome with deep gratitude these gifts, which bring to us the way of illumination, the way of life, the way of happiness.

The Shepherds

The tale of the shepherds watching over their flocks by night has also its inner meaning. The shepherds are those who are the spiritual leaders of humanity, those who have risen a little above the plane of earth, who have begun to open their spiritual vision and are trying to lead their human flocks to the hilltops of life. They are very still, these shepherds, watching, waiting, meditating, as you must watch and meditate, for if they had not been quietly communing with nature and with God they would not have been ready to receive this visitation of the angels. This is a lesson for people on earth who are mostly so busily engaged with earthly thoughts and activities that they cannot find time to enter into the silence of the spirit within, and therefore can neither hear nor see the heavenly hosts.

Try to think about this at Christmas time and do not let the material aspects of the season close your mind or your consciousness to the angelic visitors. Through the simple childlike spirit in your heart, you will be able to receive the great light which comes to the earth at Christmas time, and to perceive the visitation of the angels who will help to stimulate the growth of the Christ child in your heart.

The Angels and the Little Lights

At this time, when you are celebrating the birth of the Son of God, you hear so much about the angels coming to the shepherds; and we would remind you all of the help you could receive from the angels if only you would open your hearts to receive this blessing. When you attune yourselves, through love, to the Son, the angels are able to get their help through

to you. It is so much more difficult for them and for us
to help you when you are mentally rigid, or when you
are depressed. But if you will make the effort to
break through the bonds of the material mind, break
through that material crust, then you will find an
immediate response in the help that comes to you
from our world and from the angels. But do remember that the handle of the door is on your side.

And so at Christmas time, when you are wishing
each other a happy Christmas, we would like you to
think also of the invisible worlds and the mystic
presence which is upon the earth at this season; for
invisible hosts draw very near to the earth at
Christmas, as the Christ spirit is born anew in human
hearts. You sing carols about the coming of angels,
but you do not always stop to think about the mighty
forces which these angels bring. When you give a
Christmas party you invite all your friends, and
throw wide the door in welcome to them. We would
like you to remember your angelic and spiritual
visitors, and to throw open the door of your soul to
receive them at Christmas time. Will you remember
to do this? For angel visitors come today even as they
came to the shepherds of long ago.

Truly the Christmas festival is as old as the world
and we could tell you of ceremonies which have taken
place throughout the ages; we could tell you of sun
worship and the lighting of the little lights in the
temple. Perhaps you have not thought of the origin of
the little lights on your Christmas tree? It comes from

antiquity, and these little lights signify the light of the Sun, of the Christ, in the human heart. What is this light which lights the human heart at Christmas time? It is kindness, love. If you love, your whole being radiates light. At Christmas you think of the Son of God as a child, as a babe. He is all that— simple and loving, pure and innocent; but think of him also as that little light, the greatest gift of God to man, born in the human heart—part of that great Sun in the heavens which gives light and life to all creatures. The Son of God is both human and divine, is simple and lowly and gentle as a little babe, and infinitely great, powerful and life-giving. As the stars in the heavens are actually suns, centres of spiritual power and life, so too the earth will eventually become yet another centre of life and power and light, through the Son of God in man.

Christmas time is the season for illumination, the season for lighting the little lights in the human heart. Let the light shine! Let the light of the Christ love, the Christ spirit, shine forth from you, and you cannot fail to share in the happiness that you are all wishing each other.

Christmas in the World of Spirit

In the world of spirit Christmas time is a most grand and powerful ceremony or festival, of which man only gets a glimmering reflection. Here the presence of the Cosmic Christ is actually seen and felt. Try to

96

picture a temple, apparently built out of light, in the centre of which can be seen a Christmas tree shining with light—a symbol of the Man of Light, or the perfect light-symbol; also of the Giver of Light, the Creator. This scene is for the children, and oh! how they love their Christmas festival! Yes, spirit children are very like the earth children—they laugh, sing and dance, and are easily made happy. They hear the voices of the angels. They enjoy themselves with their appointed mother-guardians and with other children, who to them are like brothers and sisters.

Those of you who have lost loved ones, husbands, wives or children, should realise that they have only left behind the dust of the earth. They themselves are alive in this wonderful world of eternal life, about which we are trying to speak. In love there is no separation. So at your Christmas board try not to think with regret about those whom you have lost; rather let your hearts go out in joy to them in their new-found life of freedom and happiness. They can all gather round you. Yes, we are giving you their message of love. You must not think of us as being very sanctimonious and proper in the spirit world. Indeed, the beloved Lord himself has a keen sense of humour. There is greater fun in the spirit world than on earth. Therefore, may the peace of the spirit of Christ bless your Christmas, and bring to you that deep and lasting happiness which comes in the silence of the night, and in peaceful days.

*

97

Before you sleep, try to remember that if your hearts aspire, purely and simply, to join the company of heaven you too may be fetched by angels—by your own angelic teacher and guide—and so witness and even participate in this Christmas celebration. So on earth, whatever you are doing, remain alert; and in your heart keep the simple trust of a little child. We shall surely come.

The Christmas Tree

The Christmas tree is to us a symbol of the growth and development of the light of God in man, for when he hears the angel's song, when the Christ is born for him, man will develop inner powers of the spirit; he will grow in spiritual light and beauty, he will become illumined, shining with a heavenly light, even as this lighted tree sheds a circle of radiance. He will develop that radiance of spirit which has been depicted by artists as a halo of light about the head of the saint, and represented, in the symbolism of the tree, by the fairy crowning it. The lights on the tree represent the light which shines from the windows of the soul, the chakras, or centres of power, in every illumined man and woman.

The keynote of this season is joy. We beg you to maintain the spirit of Christmas. However simple and humble your gifts to each other may be, do not be too busy or too concerned with material affairs to remember these symbols of human kindness and love. Keep the spirit of Christmas with the angels in the highest heavens also. Listen in the silence of your heart to the angel voices. Obey the voice of Christ their Master, and help mankind by your own actions and way of life to understand the truth of life. Help men to realise peace within their own souls so that they may create peace on earth.

Put God into your Christmas

In wishing you a perfectly happy Christmas, we say to you, put God into everything you say and do. If you are having a happy family party, for instance, do it in the spirit of God. And we are going to say one more simple thing. When work becomes irksome, when people become a little irksome and trying, when you have to do things which are hard to do, but an inner voice is pricking you and making you do it, remember what we say now: you are doing it for God. Do it all for God. Think of God in your mind, think of the rose of divine love in your heart. Remember you can bring forth in your own self the birth of the ever-living Son of God. And with this consciousness within you, refusing to be dragged down to the material level of thought, you will indeed have a happy Christmas. If the circumstances around you cause you to feel anxious, if you will just take your hands off and keep your tongue quiet and be still and let God work His will, all will be peaceful and will work together as God wills. Be kind in your thoughts, in your judgments. Never criticise when you are assessing values. Always do it kindly.

God be in your heart and in your understanding. God be with you in your Christmas joys, in your fun, in your games, in your music, in your thoughts. Let God be your companion, in full consciousness.

We are with you at Christmas

We bring all love from the brotherhood invisible. No matter how far your travel, wherever you go, whatever you do, the friends of your spirit will be close beside you, and the happiness and joy which you feel in your hearts will be increased by their loving presence. Never shut us away at Christmas, we like to come in, we like to come into your heart and into your home.

We know many of you feel wistful about those who have passed away from your side. Yet they *are* still by your side. They have not left you; and if you can remember this during your Christmas you will lose all sense of loneliness and grief. You will know that where there is love there can be no separation. True, they are spirit; nevertheless they remain the same individuals that you loved, when in their fleshly dress. They are with you now and they will remain with you throughout your quiet, peaceful and joyous Christ mass.

A Meditation for Christmas

In the silence, in the innermost silence of the soul, man becomes aware of the birth of the Christ child.

In the silence . . . with the Star shining from above, and the angel choirs singing their song of love, peace and goodwill, the Child in *everyone* stirs.

We take you now into the garden of the spirit to a place in the form of the stable where a nativity ceremony is to be enacted.

We see the animals gathered round the cave, the stable, and the babe cradled in the arms of the divine Mother, the one who protects and loves . . . your heavenly Mother who protects and loves you.

Kneel at the crib of the Christ child. Open your heart, feel this image in your heart, see it. See the child lying in the crib, cradled like the jewel in the heart of the lotus, and worship him. . . .

Every one of you is a Christ child; your companions, you yourself, are all of the same family, born in the same way—tiny sparks of the great light, born humbly in a stable, surrounded by the zodiac, the animals in the stable. Ponder on the symbolism of this beautiful story and understand that the birth of the Christ is the most wonderful event which has ever happened on earth.

Banish, if you will, all old-fashioned orthodoxy

101

and church-ianity, but remember the truth of the birth of the Christ child on earth, for without the miracle of His birth there would be no life on this planet.

Our Christmas message to you is this: may you all, every one of you, understand the eternal truth of the Christ birth, because it will make you truly happy. It will make you happy because you will realise how wonderful is the gift of life and that it is eternal.

Take the days as they come, take the seasons as they come and go, for they too continue for ever and ever and ever. But as you grow in understanding and spiritual quality and strength you will enter into ever more perfect life.

*

Come let us worship him. . . .

Now we see the Christ in a blazing aura. Oh, so glorious is the light around him! And in the very centre of this light see that gentle Man – Woman, that gentle Being, the perfect dual soul, the Child of God . . . born to you, born in you at the Christ mass.

The New Year: Au Revoir

IT IS customary at the beginning of each year for kindly people to wish each other happiness, or 'good luck' (though we know that there is really no such thing as good or bad luck). But what do we mean by happiness? Will satisfaction of our material desires and longings bring us happiness? If every material or even spiritual desire is fulfilled, will this bring us a happy New Year?

We do not think you will find this to be so. Happiness is not merely pleasure, for happiness can come sometimes in the midst of great sorrow. Happiness, my friends, is the realisation of God in the heart. Happiness is the result of praise, of thanksgiving, of faith, of acceptance; a quiet, tranquil realisation of the love of God. This brings to the soul perfect and indescribable happiness. God is happiness.

And so, my dear friends, we do not wish you good luck, we do not wish you prosperity, we do not wish you good health . . . we wish you supreme happiness in the union of your spirit with the Great White Light, with Christ, and all His angels. We wish you the happiness of heaven, for no earthly event will ever rob you of this. Not birth, nor death, nor sorrow can rob you of this true happiness of becoming at one with our Father–Mother God.

And so may you find this happiness in the New Year, and may you be able to sow a little seed, or shed a little light onto the pathway of another and thus share your happiness with your brother.